You Are Unique and You Can Achieve Anything!:

Inspirational Stories about Strong and Wonderful Girls Just Like You

Inspired Inner Genius

This book belongs to the

wonderful

....

Here at Inspired Inner Genius, we believe that every child is born a genius.

Join us in our journey to inspire the world, one child at a time.

Written by Jane Alcott · Published by Inspired Inner Genius
Cover designed by Menna Eissa

Free Bonus

Grab the first two eBooks of our flagship Inspired Inner Genius series for free.

Simply visit: https://go.inspiredinnergenius.com/ebook or scan the QR code below to grab two inspirational biography books for your little one(s)!

Table of Contents

Introduction

A special greeting to our precious young reader,

First of all, a very big thank you for picking up this book and giving it a read.

We at Inspired Inner Genius truly believe that the future lies in your young but capable hands.

We believe that you are a remarkable individual who has the power to change the world!

Because of this, we have put together this compilation of stories that we believe will empower you to make an impact on the world, starting from those around you.

This book that you hold in your hands has been written, packaged, and published delicately with an abundance of love and care.

In it contains 11 spectacular tales that cover topics ranging from friendship and forgiveness to dreams and passion. As we dive into each of these stories, we hope that you will be able to relate to the characters and situations. Moreover, we hope that you will draw upon the lessons to apply them to your own lives.

Not only that, we hope that you will discover and be reminded that you are unique, special, and very much capable of achieving your dreams!

Through this book, we hope to impart to you some of our biggest takeaways that we believe will equip you with the values to make a positive impact on the world.

We sincerely hope that you will enjoy this book as much as we enjoyed creating it specially for YOU.

Well, don't just take our word for it. Dive into the book and find out for yourself!

Without further ado, here are 11 beautiful stories that we hope will touch your heart...

-- The Inspired Inner Genius Team

1: Maisie and the Piano

Maisie didn't want to play the piano.

The air was filled with her brother Seb's perfect playing, and that just made things worse. His notes sounded so perfect and his song was so smooth and fast. Maisie wished she could play like that, but even "Twinkle Twinkle Little Star" was too hard for her. Her fingers got tripped up over each other, and after playing the wrong note at the same part over and over again, she had quit and stormed off to lie on her favorite fluffy rug in the living room.

Seb said he could help her, but Maisie didn't want help from her big brother. She wanted to be able to play on her own. She wanted to sound as good as he did!

"Maisie? What are you doing down there?" her mom asked as she walked into the living room.

"I can't play the piano," Maisie said sadly with her face buried in the fluffy carpet.

"Why not?"

"It's too hard."

Mom sat down beside her. "I'm sure Seb would help you if you asked nicely."

Maisie flipped over onto her back and crossed her arms, frowning at her mom. "I don't want help."

"Honey," Mom said. "You won't get better if you don't play."

"I don't want to play. Piano is too hard." That was just the problem. She really *did* want to play, but her songs just didn't sound good enough.

Mom spoke softly. "You may not play the same way as Seb, but that's okay. You have your own way of doing things that's just as special."

But as Seb's beautiful song continued, Maisie knew she could never be that good. She stood up to get some proof. Marching off to the playroom, she brought back two pieces of paper for her mother to see.

"Look," Maisie said, holding up the two papers. "Here's my drawing, and here's Seb's. His is much better than mine."

Mom smiled. "But how can you say that when you used different colors and shapes? They're different pictures, and they're both beautiful."

Maisie looked at the two drawings. Seb had drawn a red race car, while she had drawn a green boat on the ocean. They *were* very different drawings, and she liked boats better than race cars, anyway.

"Let's go play the piano," Mom said. "I don't know how to play songs, but I hope you can show me."

Maisie smiled. "We can play together!"

As Seb finished his song, Mom asked if they could have a turn. He agreed and packed up his music.

"Seb?" Maisie said as she got up on the piano bench. "Your song was really beautiful."

Seb smiled. "Thank you!"

Mom got up on the bench too. "Can we play 'Twinkle Twinkle Little Star?'" she asked.

Maisie shook her head. "Let's play something else."

Maisie showed her mom how to play some notes on the piano. She then played her favorite song called "Sailing." The notes came out perfect! When she finished, her mother clapped.

"That sounded so beautiful! Can I hear another one?"

So Maisie played another song. And another. And another! She had forgotten just how much music she knew. Maybe she *could* play piano well!

But as she flipped to the next page in her music book, she saw the notes for "Twinkle Twinkle Little Star." She thought that maybe she should give up again. However many times she had tried, she just couldn't play it!

But she had just played so many beautiful songs with the same fingers and keys. If she could do that, then why couldn't she play this song?

Maisie sat up and lifted her fingers above the keys. "I can play it." And she began.

Even if there was a little pause before her usual mistake, the song still sounded just like it was supposed to. Maisie couldn't believe that she was playing beautiful music just like Seb!

When the song was over, Maisie smiled and cheered. "I did it! I said I could play it, and I did!"

"That's right!" Mom said, hugging her. "The only limit to what you can do is yourself. If you believe it, you can do it. That was the best version of 'Twinkle Twinkle Little Star' that I've ever heard."

Maisie looked at the scoresheet again. It didn't seem so hard anymore.

"Can I hear an encore?" Maisie's mom asked.

Maisie frowned. "What's an encore?"

"It's when you play another song because the last one was so good!"

Maisie grinned and turned the page. She had only just started practicing the next song, but it couldn't be too much harder than "Twinkle Twinkle Little Star."

"I can play it," she said.

And play it, she did.

Moral of the Story

Even though Maisie was good at playing the piano, she didn't want to play because she was comparing herself to her brother and didn't think she sounded as good as him. Remember that you are one-of-a-kind, the only you there's ever been! You may not do something the same as someone else, but it doesn't mean that your way is wrong. Keep trying, believe in yourself, and you can do anything!

2: Olivia's Facts

Olivia loved to know facts. She liked every subject: fish, games, airplanes, baking, and more. She wanted to know everything about the world.

When Olivia went to the library, she liked to close her eyes and let her mom or dad take her to any section. After Olivia opened her eyes, she would pick a book from that section and read it, writing down facts along the way.

Mrs. Feathers, Olivia's teacher, loved that she knew so many facts. When Olivia came into school on Monday mornings, she always told Mrs. Feathers about the facts that she had learned over the weekend.

Because she was too busy learning about facts, Olivia didn't have many friends.

Olivia used to have a friend in her class named Angelina Muff. But one time, Olivia told Angelina a fact about how eating too much sugar was not good for her when she saw that Angelina had five cookies in her lunchbox. Angelina did not like this.

So now, there was no one but Mrs. Feathers to listen to Olivia's facts. She wished that she could have a classmate to talk to, but she was happy to have Mrs. Feathers.

Then, one day, something special happened.

In the middle of the year, Olivia walked into her classroom and noticed that something was different. There were seventeen desks instead of sixteen!

"Mrs. Feathers?" said Olivia, walking up to her teacher's desk. "Why is there an extra desk?"

Mrs. Feathers smiled. "We're getting a new student in our class, Olivia, and I think you will like her."

Olivia felt excited. When she went back to her desk, she saw that the new student's desk was right next to hers!

While she waited to meet the new student, Olivia took out the animal magazine she was reading and started learning about gorillas.

"Is that a silverback gorilla on the cover?" a voice asked.

Olivia looked up at a girl with blonde hair and two pigtails. She knew it must be the new student.

"Yes, it is," Olivia said with a smile. She turned the magazine sideways. "Do you want to share?"

"Yes, I would love to!" The girl smiled. "I'm Mary."

"I'm Olivia." Olivia smiled back. "Did you know that silverbacks have almost the same exact DNA as people?"

Mary nodded. "Yes, I did! And they're very smart, too."

By the time class began that day, Olivia and Mary were best friends. Olivia was glad to finally have someone to share facts with, but she still wished that Mary wasn't the only one she could talk to.

One day, Mrs. Feathers gave the class a project. Everyone had to make a poster with a theme, like animals, food, or cars. The poster would have pictures and facts about the theme on it, and everyone could choose one person to do the project with.

"Maybe our project can be on bugs!" Mary said. Of course, she and Olivia were partners.

Olivia frowned. "I don't like bugs very much. Maybe the ocean?"

Mary shook her head. "I'm afraid of the ocean."

While they discussed what theme to do, Percy Evans, a boy in their class, walked up to Olivia's desk.

"Hi," he said, looking down at the floor. "Can you help Dalia and me find some facts about flowers?"

Olivia knew that she could say no to Percy. This was the first time he had ever talked to her.

But her dad always said to be kind to others, even when they didn't understand you. So Olivia smiled and said, "Yes, I can! I have a book about flowers in my backpack right now."

Percy smiled too. Olivia got her book and sat down with Percy and Dalia. Another group asked Mary for her help finding facts about caterpillars, and she was more than happy to help. Soon, Olivia and Mary found themselves helping the whole class with facts! The whole classroom was filled with laughter and chatter. At her desk, Mrs. Feathers smiled.

When the day of the project came, everyone had beautiful posters with lots of good facts. They all thanked Olivia and Mary, and the two fact-lovers never felt like outsiders again.

Moral of the Story

Olivia felt like she didn't fit in with her class at school. Sometimes, you may feel like you're different from everyone else, too. But your talents are special, and you can use them to help people just like Olivia did! If you are kind, you will always find a friend, just like how Olivia became friends with Mary, and eventually with the rest of her class.

3: The Librarian

Amelia loved the library. She liked the books, how quiet it was, and the soft purple carpet they had for kids to sit on. She went to the library after school almost every day to do her homework.

But there was one thing that Amelia didn't like about the library: the librarian.

Sometimes, when Amelia was looking at books, the librarian would ask Amelia if she needed help. She was a very tall woman with gray hair and pointed glasses. Amelia never knew what to say to her, so she always ran away to her mom.

When Amelia turned eight, her mom told her to try checking out her books from the library counter by herself. But when Amelia saw the librarian at the big checkout desk, she shook her head and gave her books back to her mom.

"Okay, honey, we can try next time," her mom said. Amelia waited off to the side while her mom checked out the books.

But every time they went to the library, Amelia was still too afraid to check out her own books.

One day, Amelia's mom had to carry Jennifer, Amelia's baby sister, into the library with them.

"But Mom," Amelia said, "if Jennifer cries, the librarian might come and tell her to be quiet."

"It will be okay," her mom said. "Besides, Jennifer is asleep."

Amelia went off to look for the next books in the series she was currently reading. When she found them, she took them back to her mom to be checked out.

Then, Jennifer started crying.

Amelia immediately looked around for the librarian. She hid behind her mom and didn't look up.

"Amelia, I have to go change Jennifer," her mom said. "You can check out your books, and then wait for me at one of the tables. We have to go as soon as I'm done so that we can meet your dad for dinner." She smiled at Amelia and gave her the library card. "You can do it."

Amelia stood still. Her books suddenly felt very heavy. She looked up at the desk and saw the librarian helping someone check out a stack of big books. Her mom gave her a hug and then walked to the bathroom.

Amelia didn't know what to do. She could wait for her mom to come back, but what if that made them late for dinner? Amelia didn't want that.

She looked down at the shiny blue library card in her hand. When she looked back up, she saw a little boy at the counter. The librarian was smiling and talking to him, and he was smiling too!

Amelia thought that if that little boy could talk to the librarian, then she could too. She got behind the little boy in line, and as soon as he walked away, she set her books on the counter.

"Hello, dear," the librarian said. Her voice actually sounded very kind. "May I please have your library card?"

Amelia nodded and placed the card down next to the books. She was still afraid to look at the librarian.

"You know," the librarian said, "you can get your own library card. You could check out more books."

Amelia decided to look at the librarian as she spoke, because her mom had told her it was polite. The librarian's green eyes sparkled with happiness.

"Really?" Amelia asked.

"Really!" The librarian scanned the books and stacked them all up again. She then handed Amelia a piece of paper. "Show that to your mother and see what she thinks." As she handed back the books, she touched the one on top. "This is the best book in the series!"

Amelia grinned. "You've read them! I love these books!"

The librarian smiled. "They're some of my favorites."

Amelia took the books from the counter. "Thank you," she remembered to say.

"You're welcome. Have a nice day, dear. I'll see you next time!"

Amelia waved and walked away with her books. She had done it! And she was never afraid of the librarian again.

Moral of the Story

Amelia was afraid to talk to the librarian and check out books on her own. When she finally tried to do it by herself, she found out that the librarian was actually really nice and even made a new friend. It may be scary to try new things or make new friends, but that doesn't mean that you can't be brave, too! Have courage, and you will learn new things and make precious friends that you otherwise wouldn't have if you didn't try!

4: Rachel's Choice

Rachel could smell cookies baking. She was in the middle of playing with her favorite dolls, but she put them down and followed her nose to the kitchen, where her dad was washing the dishes.

Rachel sneaked behind him and peered into the oven. Inside, she could see two pans of dough starting to spread out into cookies.

"Dad?" she asked. "When will the cookies be ready?"

Rachel's dad jumped in surprise and turned around. "I didn't even know you were there!"

Rachel giggled. Her dad wiped his hands on a towel and looked into the oven.

"Those cookies aren't for us," he said. "They're for Evan to take to his class tomorrow."

Rachel frowned as she thought of her little brother getting all of those cookies. "Why does Evan get them?"

"It's Sharing Day in his class tomorrow. He needs to have enough for everyone in his class."

The smell got stronger and Rachel's stomach felt empty. "I can't just eat one?"

Dad shook his head. "How about this? I'll bake some more tomorrow that will be just for us!"

Rachel looked back at the oven. She wanted the cookies *now*.

"Come on," her dad said. "Let's go play a game."

Rachel went to play a board game with Mom, Dad and Evan, but the whole time, she kept smelling the cookies. When they were done, her dad got up and took them out of the oven. The sweet, warm smell filled the whole house!

"Don't worry," Mom said when she saw Rachel's sad face. "We will make your favorite cookies tomorrow: oatmeal chocolate chip!"

Rachel smiled, but cookies tomorrow weren't the same thing as cookies today.

As her dad started doing his Sunday afternoon cleaning and her mom went upstairs to talk on the phone, Rachel played with Evan. He was two whole years younger than her and still in kindergarten. Why should he get cookies and not her?

"I'm excited about school tomorrow," he said as he raced a toy car around the carpet.

"*I* would be excited if *I* had a lot of cookies."

"Maybe you'll have Sharing Day in your class one day too!"

Evan played and smiled at the thought of giving cookies to his class. Rachel felt guilty for wanting to eat one, but she kept looking at the kitchen anyway. After she finished playing with Evan, she got up to go look at the cookies again. They were still warm, sitting out on the counter to cool. Rachel wanted one more than ever.

She looked around. No one was watching. No one would know if she took one.

But if she ate a cookie, then one person in Evan's class wouldn't have one. That wouldn't be very fair.

So Rachel took one last sniff of the cookies and went back to play with Evan.

A little while later, Mom and Dad wanted to talk to her. Rachel loved going into her parents' room because they had a big bed with soft pillows and covers. She jumped onto the bed giggling, and Mom and Dad sat next to her.

"Thank you for letting Evan have his cookies today, Rachel," Dad said. "I know it was hard for you not to eat one, but Evan is really excited about giving them to his class."

Rachel sighed. "I almost ate one when no one was looking," she said. She got a pillow and hugged it, feeling worse than ever.

"But you didn't," her mom said softly. "Do you know what that means? It means that you are honest and strong."

Rachel sat up. She had never thought of it as being strong before. She smiled. "Really?"

Dad nodded. "You are a very strong, kind girl, Rachel. And that's why, for our dessert tonight, we're going out for ice cream."

Rachel was so excited that she got off the bed and did a dance. Mom and Dad laughed.

That night, Rachel got into her car seat and buckled herself in as quickly as she could. As her family drove to the ice cream store, she forgot all about the smell of the baking cookies. Instead, she had fun with her family and ate a yummy ice cream treat that she decided was even better than a cookie.

Moral of the Story

Rachel really wanted to take a cookie, even though she knew that they were for her brother Evan. When she chose to be strong, be honest, and follow the rules, she felt good and her parents even rewarded her for it! You will always have a chance to make a good choice or a bad choice. Good choices will make you feel happy and proud of yourself, but bad choices will make you feel sad and maybe even disappointed in yourself. Always think carefully before making a choice - you never know when you will make or ruin your own day!

5: A New Friend

Nora Jones and Jorge Diaz always played together at the park. Their parents took them there at least three times a week because they had so much fun together.

They created imaginary games, timed how quickly they could go down the slide, and compared who could swing the highest. Nora and Jorge were best friends, and they always had been.

"What are we going to play today?" Jorge asked one afternoon at the park. There was a chilly breeze, so they both wore fuzzy jackets.

"Let's play house," Nora said. "The playground will be our house, and the slide will be our front door!"

This sounded good to both of them, so they started their game where they would pretend to be adults. Jorge went under the playground and pretended to be in an office talking to people on the phone and typing on a computer. Nora pet an imaginary cat and sent an imaginary daughter off to school. Soon, they had a party at their imaginary house with lots of pretend people, food, and music.

A girl with two red braids walked onto the playground where Jorge and Nora were having their party. "My name is Liv," she said. "Can I come to the party too?"

"You're standing on the table!" Nora said, even though the table was just imaginary.

Liv looked down and took a step back. "I'm sorry, I didn't see it there."

"The party is only for guests," Nora said. "Do you have an invitation?"

Liv frowned. "I don't think I do."

"It's pretend," Jorge whispered.

Nora frowned at Jorge. He was smiling at the girl. Did he like her better than Nora?

"Sorry," Nora said to Liv. "If you don't have an invitation, you can't join."

Liv hung her head. "Oh. I'm sorry." She walked away to the other side of the playground.

Jorge looked just as sad as Liv did. "Why didn't you let her play with us?"

Nora didn't feel like she was having fun anymore. For years, it had just been her and Jorge playing together. She didn't want anyone else to play with them.

"She's never played with us before," Nora said. "She wouldn't know how to do it."

Jorge didn't look like he was having fun either.

"Let's keep playing," Nora said. The house party kept going, but it was different than before. Jorge kept looking at Liv on the other side of the playground. Nora couldn't use her imagination very well.

At the end of the day, Jorge didn't look at her when he said goodbye. That night, Nora felt very bad as she lay in her bed. She didn't like making Jorge sad and she knew she hadn't been nice to Liv.

When Nora went to the park again in two days, she was surprised to see that Jorge was already playing with Liv. They were laughing like they were best friends as they played on the swings. Jorge saw Nora and waved. Nora crossed her arms and stomped back to her parents. She sat down on a bench and said that she wanted to go home.

As her mom was tucking her into bed that night, Nora cried and said that she never wanted to go back to the park.

"Why not?" her mom asked.

"Jorge doesn't like me anymore. He has a new friend."

"I saw him wave to you today," she said. "You and Jorge have been playing together since you were very little. I know that he still likes you."

Nora shook her head. "He was playing with his new friend instead of me." She sniffed as she kept crying.

"Did you ask if you could play with them?"

Nora thought of how she treated Liv when she asked to play. If Nora asked Jorge and Liv to play, they would treat her the same way, and she didn't want that. "No. They'll be mean to me."

"Has Jorge ever been mean to you?"

Nora thought and thought, but she couldn't think of one time where Jorge had been mean to her. "No," she said.

"I think you should talk to him. We'll go to the park again tomorrow." Her mom kissed her on the head and said goodnight.

The next day, Nora wasn't looking forward to the park for the first time ever. At the park, Liv and Jorge were already playing. Jorge waved at her like he did last time. Nora walked over to them and looked at the ground, holding her hands in front of her.

"I'm sorry for being mean," she said. "Can I play with you?"

"I forgive you," Liv said with a smile. "We're pretending to be kings and queens."

"I love that game!" Nora said.

"I'm really glad that you're playing with us," Jorge said. Nora realized that she was silly for thinking that he didn't like her anymore.

Nora, Jorge, and Liv all started playing at the park together after that day, and they were all best friends.

Moral of the Story

Nora really liked playing with her friend Jorge. She didn't want to play with someone new, so she was mean to Liv. But when she was bold enough to admit that she was wrong, her friends forgave her. Also, when meeting new people, you might not want to be nice to them or let them play with you sometimes. But when you are kind and accepting of them, you might just make a new best friend like Nora did!

6: The Sleepover

It was Friday night at Jade's house. This was Jade's favorite night of the week because it meant she got to watch a movie with her mom.

Jade started to feel excited when her mom put popcorn into the microwave. She could hardly wait as she got the ice cream from the freezer.

After they had all of the snacks ready, Jade and her mom sat on the couch. They put on one of Jade's favorite movies and started eating while they watched. Jade got to stay up late, which was one of her favorite parts about Fridays.

Jade and her mom clapped at the end of the movie. Then, Jade's mom tucked her in and read her a story before bed. It was the perfect night.

The next morning, Jade was still excited.

She had a sleepover that night at her friend Tia's house. She had never been to a sleepover before, and she was a little scared, but mostly excited. So excited, in fact, that she could hardly do anything but jump up and down all day.

Jade started to get a little scared again as her mom helped her pack for the sleepover. Her mom told her not to be afraid because it was fun to get to see what a friend's house was like.

When Jade saw Tia's mom arrive in her car, she wasn't afraid anymore. Saying goodbye to her mom, she ran out the door to give Tia a hug. They got in the car and Tia's mom drove them to Tia's house. All the way there, Tia and Jade talked about what they were going to do that night.

"I hope you like lasagna, Jade," Tia's mom said. "Mr. James is a good cook and he's making some."

Jade started to feel hungry. "I don't think I've ever had lasagna before." Her mom mostly made chicken or frozen dinners, which was always good.

When they got inside the house, Tia's little brother and sister ran to the door to say hello. Jade laughed as Tia's sister, Mya, held onto her leg and wouldn't let go.

As they walked into the house, Jade smelled something amazing.

"Hi, Jade!" Mr. James, Tia's dad, said. He was in the kitchen getting some plates. "I hope you're hungry!"

"I am!" Jade exclaimed. Tia showed her to her room, which was painted pink and filled with sparkly things.

"Wow!" Jade said. "I wish my room was this big!"

Jade set her sleepover bag down and followed Tia to the dining room. Tia's whole family sat at the table to eat.

Lasagna was the best thing that Jade had ever tasted. She ate it so quickly that Tia laughed. Her brother Mason tried to eat just as quickly as Jade and made a mess! Dinner was so delicious and fun that Jade was smiling the whole time.

After dinner, Jade went back up to Tia's room where they made bracelets, braided each other's hair, and painted on some things that Tia's mom called "canvases." Later on, Tia's parents brought them hot brownies and ice cream.

It was the best night ever.

After wolfing down their dessert, Tia and Jade talked for a long time. Finally, Tia fell asleep. Jade took a little longer getting to bed. She kept thinking about how much fun she'd had at Tia's house.

Then, she remembered that she had to go back home the next day. At home, there was only Mom. Jade loved her mom, but Tia had a mom, a dad, and siblings! Her dad cooked, and their house had a lot of space to play in. Jade didn't have that in her apartment.

Suddenly, Jade wished very much that she could live with Tia.

The next morning, Jade cheered up as Mr. James prepared pancakes and bacon ready for breakfast. Then, Tia and Jade played with Mason and Mya in the living room.

When the doorbell rang, Jade felt like it was the end of the world. She knew it was time to go home and she felt tears in her eyes. She didn't want to go back. She wanted to stay with Tia.

Jade didn't want to cry in front of everyone, so she hid her tears and pretended she didn't hear the doorbell. Instead, she kept playing with Tia.

"Hi, honey," Jade's mom said as she walked up behind her. "Did you have a good time?"

Jade nodded, not looking up at her mom.

"It's time for us to go, sweetie. Tia's family has things to do today."

Jade stopped and turned to look up at her mom. "Can't I at least stay for a little bit longer?"

Her mom smiled sadly. "I'm sorry, honey. Maybe Tia's parents will let you come over another time."

"Of course we will," said Tia's mom.

"Tomorrow?" Jade asked excitedly.

Everyone laughed, but Jade was serious.

Jade got in the car with her mom and stared out the window on the way home. Her mom tried to ask her questions about the sleepover, but she only gave short answers.

"What's wrong, honey?" her mom asked when they got home. "Are you sad about leaving Tia's?"

Jade nodded. "Her room is a lot bigger than mine, and she has a big family, a big house, and good food."

Her mom smiled. "It's called 'envy' when you want someone else's things. But do you know what? I was feeling envious too when I came to pick you up from Tia's house."

Jade's eyes widened. "Really?"

"Yes. It's easy to want what somebody else has. But remember, Jade, that we have a lot of special things too."

"Like our movie nights?"

"Yes! Can you think of anything else?"

Jade thought. "My bed, and your special chicken dish, and the kitty that comes to the window every morning!"

Her mom laughed. "Those are all very good things to be thankful for. You don't need somebody else's things to be happy, Jade. Everything you need is right here."

Jade smiled. If she was at Tia's house all the time, she would miss so many things from her own home.

"I am thankful, Mama. And most of all, I'm thankful for you!" She hugged her mom tightly. And just then, she didn't miss Tia's house anymore. She had everything she needed right there.

Moral of the Story

Jade was envious of everything her friend Tia had and she forgot about all of the great things she had herself. Your family, your room, your stuff, and the way you look may be different than what other people have, but that's okay! Don't let envy make you forget to be thankful for all the precious things that you already have.

7: The Vacation

Today was the day: vacation day!

Paige was so excited that she couldn't even sleep. She was wide awake before the sun rose, thinking about all the things that her family would do in their cabin in the mountains. It was going to be so much fun!

When she heard noise from downstairs, Paige jumped out of bed and went down the staircase. She saw her dad in the kitchen making coffee. He laughed as she zoomed in.

"You're up early."

"When are we leaving?" Paige asked, jumping up and down.

"As soon as we can get everything packed up in the car."

Paige grinned, then looked at his coffee. "Can I have a sip?"

Dad sighed, then held out the cup. "Just *one* sip."

Paige took a big gulp, swallowed it down, then giggled.

"With that energy, I hope you're going to help me pack the trunk!" Dad said.

"Okay!"

Soon enough, Tom, Paige's older brother, was awake too. Paige's mom walked around making sure she had everything packed. Paige was busy carrying small things to the car. She handed them to Dad, who packed it all away neatly.

Just as the sun started rising, they were ready to go. Tom was barely awake and fell back asleep as soon as he got in the car. Paige brought her stuffed bear, Teddy, along with her.

As the car drove through the city, Paige asked questions about what they were going to do on vacation. Tom told her to be quiet, but she didn't listen. How could he be asleep at a time like this?

Paige kept talking to her parents and Teddy as she looked out the window. She liked watching everything change outside. It was her favorite thing to do in the car.

"Be quiet!" Tom shushed at her.

Paige stuck out her tongue at him and held Teddy tighter. Tom stuck out his tongue back and fell asleep again. He pulled his hat down over his head to cover his eyes.

"Maybe we should just be quiet for a little bit, Paige. It's still early," Mom called out from the front.

Paige sighed. "Okay." She was quiet for a few minutes, but she couldn't contain her excitement any longer.

She held Teddy in front of her and started whispering to him. She told him facts about the mountains and how cold it would be. She told him that they would be high up, but he didn't need to be scared.

As she talked, Paige felt a tug on her braid. "Ow!" she said.

Tom pretended like he was still asleep, but Paige knew better. He had pulled her hair.

"Mom, Tom pulled my hair."

"Your mother's asleep, honey," Dad remarked as he drove. "Let's keep it down for a little bit. And Tom, don't disturb your sister. Keep your hands to yourself."

Tom didn't say anything. Paige glared angrily at him.

A little while went by and nothing happened. Then, Paige felt someone kick her seat. When she turned around, Tom still looked sound asleep. She turned back to the window. It happened again, but Tom still pretended like he hadn't moved.

"Stop it!" Paige exclaimed.

"Sweetie," her dad whispered. "Shhh, your mom and Tom are still asleep."

"Tom keeps kicking my seat and Teddy doesn't like it," she said, holding up the teddy bear.

"Tom," Dad sighed, "we're about to make a quick stop. We're going to have a talk when we get out of the car."

Tom looked mad. He threw his hat in between their seats and crossed his arms. Paige smiled because she knew he was getting in trouble. He deserved it.

Her dad stopped the car and he and Tom got out. Paige's mom said they should go to the bathroom. Before Paige got out of the car, she saw Tom's hat sitting in between the seats. She looked, and no one was watching, so she took the hat and held it behind her back.

Tom had been mean to her all morning, so now she was going to be mean to him.

"Paige," Mom said, "why do you have Tom's hat?"

Paige stood very still. She thought that her mom couldn't see it. She looked down at the ground.

"Paige?"

"I was going to throw it in the trash can," Paige said. She could feel tears in her eyes. Now she was going to get in trouble, even though it wasn't her fault.

Mom knelt down beside her. "That's not a very kind thing to do," she said.

Paige crossed her arms. "Tom was mean to me! It makes me feel so mad!"

"Do you think it will make things better if you do mean things to Tom because he did them to you?"

"He deserves it," Paige said, starting to cry. "And now I'm in trouble!"

"You're not in trouble." Mom stood up and hugged her. "It's okay that you're angry, Paige. Everybody gets mad sometimes."

Paige sniffed. "But you never get mad."

"Yes I do," Mom said. "But when you try to be mean to someone who was mean to you, it only makes things worse. So, do you know what I do instead?"

Paige shook her head.

"When I get really mad, I walk away from whoever made me mad and I talk to someone about my feelings. Then, I try to talk to the person who made me angry and we figure things out. I immediately feel better, and no one else gets hurt."

That sounded like a good idea, but Paige didn't know if she could do that. "That sounds hard."

"It is hard, Paige, but you have already done it. You told me how you feel." Mom smiled sweetly at her. "What do you want to do with Tom's hat?

Paige looked at the hat, then looked back at the car. She realized that she didn't really feel mad anymore. "I want to give it back to him."

Mom smiled. "You are such a brave, strong girl, Paige. I want to be more like you."

Paige grinned. She felt so much better that she ran back to the car and gave Tom his hat back right then.

"You made me really mad when you kept kicking my seat and pulling my hair," Paige said.

"I'm sorry," Tom said, and he meant it. "I got mad because you kept talking."

"I'm sorry too." Paige smiled. Mom was right. She didn't feel mad at all anymore.

Moral of the Story

Paige got really mad when her big brother Tom was teasing her. Because of her anger, she almost threw away his hat. Even when you get really angry, you don't have to hurt anyone or say mean words. You can talk about how angry you feel and walk away from the person who is making you angry. You may still feel mad, but after a little while, you'll feel better. And, just like Paige did, you can forgive the person who made you mad and still be friends with them!

8: Bonnie and Carter

Bonnie skipped into her classroom on a Wednesday morning with her blue lunchbox. She was very excited to eat the big sandwich and chips that her aunt had packed for her. She always made the best sandwiches.

After putting her backpack and lunchbox away, Bonnie went to go sit at her desk. All of the desks in the classroom were arranged in twos. That meant when she sat down, she was facing Carter. She hadn't talked to Carter very much before their desks were put together. Now, they were good friends.

Carter smiled as she sat down. "I got to stay up late and watch a movie with my big brother last night!" he said.

"Wow!" Bonnie said. "My aunt made pizza. She let me spin the dough in the air!"

Carter laughed as Bonnie showed him how she had spun the dough. Then their teacher, Mr. Roberts, started the day and Bonnie and Carter stayed quiet so they could learn.

When Mr. Roberts said it was time for lunch, Bonnie got really excited again.

"My aunt makes the best sandwiches in the whole wide world!" she told Carter. "I can't wait to eat it."

"I have chicken salad," Carter replied. Bonnie laughed at the silly face he made.

"Will you save me a spot next to you at lunch while I go to the bathroom?" Bonnie asked Carter.

"Sure!"

Bonnie left her lunchbox with Mr. Roberts while she went to the bathroom. When she came back, she took the lunchbox and went to find Carter at their usual table. She stopped when she saw that it was packed full.

There were several other boys from her class sitting with Carter. They were laughing and talking about video games. But Carter had said he would save a spot for her!

Bonnie shyly walked up to the table. She didn't know any of the other boys.

"Carter," she said, "there isn't room for me." She didn't know what else to say.

The boys around Carter laughed at Bonnie. Carter looked down like he didn't know what to do.

"Sorry," he said. "I want to talk to other people today. I'll sit with you another day, okay?"

Bonnie felt her eyes fill with tears. She gave one mean look at Carter and ran away, sitting and eating lunch by herself. She didn't even think about how good her sandwich tasted.

When they got back to class, Carter sat at his desk quietly. He looked at Bonnie, but Bonnie did not look at him. She didn't talk to him all day or even say goodbye when school was over.

All that night, Bonnie felt miserable. Was Carter not her friend anymore? Why had he not kept his promise?

The next day, Bonnie walked up to Mr. Roberts' desk in the morning. "Mr. Roberts, can my desk be moved away from Carter?"

Mr. Roberts looked surprised. "Why would you want that?"

Bonnie told him what had happened the day before at lunch.

"Hm," Mr. Roberts said when she was done. "That must have made you upset, but you can forgive Carter and still be friends."

"I don't want to forgive him," Bonnie said. "He was mean, and everyone laughed at me!"

"I will see if I can move you soon then, but it won't be today."

Bonnie sighed and sat back down at her desk. She looked away from Carter.

"Bonnie, I'm really sorry about yesterday."

Bonnie pretended not to hear him. Sorry wasn't good enough; he should have kept his promise.

Two more days passed and Bonnie felt worse than ever as she sat down across from Carter that morning. She wanted to play with him again and sit with him at lunch, but she was still mad at him.

Bonnie thought of what Mr. Roberts had said. Her aunt always said that forgiveness was hard, but important.

Even if it would be hard to forgive Carter, Bonnie decided that she would rather do it than never talk to him again.

"Bonnie," Carter said, "will we ever be friends again?"

Finally, Bonnie looked at Carter. "You broke your promise," she said.

Carter nodded. "I should not have done that. I'm really sorry."

"I forgive you." As Bonnie said those words, the sadness she had been feeling started to fade away.

Carter smiled. "Really? Thank you, Bonnie! I won't ever break a promise again. I promise."

Bonnie laughed. "And I promise to be better at forgiveness."

And both of them kept their promises.

Moral of the Story

Bonnie was very sad when her friend Carter didn't let her sit at the lunch table with him. She didn't want to forgive him, and that made her feel bad as the days passed. But once she forgave Carter, she felt a lot better and they were able to be friends again. Forgiveness is very hard sometimes. You may want to stay angry at someone that was mean to you, but you will be happier once you forgive. If you had wronged someone else, wouldn't you want them to forgive you too?

9: The Best Breakfast

Sarah woke up to the sounds of nature. Birds were chirping. Water was running. Even the bugs were noisy.

Sarah loved camping. She went camping a lot with her sisters and her parents. She liked sitting by the fire and hearing her mom play the guitar. She also liked eating food from the grill and sleeping in a tent.

So Sarah woke up happy, and she was looking forward to breakfast. Her dad was making bacon and pancakes, and they would have hot chocolate too! That was always Sarah's favorite part.

When everyone was awake, Mom began making the fire while her dad started getting breakfast ready. It was cold out, which made the warm fire feel even more cozy. Sarah sat by and grinned as she watched her mom stoke it.

"Make it as high as it can go, Mom!" she cheered.

Sarah's sisters, Juliet and Louise, sat beside her on a great big log. Once the fire was going, their mom told them to watch it while she visited the bathroom. She had to walk a few minutes away from the campsite to get there.

"I'll watch it, Mom! I won't let the forest catch fire!" said Sarah.

"You just said you wanted to make a huge fire!" Louise rolled her eyes. Juliet just laughed.

Meanwhile, Dad was just about done with making breakfast. The pancakes smelled so good. He even put blueberries in them! Sarah saw him get out the maple syrup and her stomach growled like a bear.

When Sarah's mom came back into camp, she started talking quietly to dad.

"What do you think they are saying?" Juliet asked, watching them whisper.

"I don't know," said Louise.

Sarah checked the fire. She had been watching it earnestly, and the forest wasn't on fire yet. "I hope it isn't about the fire," she said to herself.

After a few minutes, Mom and Dad walked over, both with smiles.

"Girls," Mom called out to them, "there's a family with one little girl a few campsites over. I met her mom on my walk. Their water cooler leaked and got all over their food, so now they don't have anything to eat for breakfast. Do you think we can share our breakfast with them?"

"Yes!" Juliet immediately exclaimed. She was always excited to meet new people.

"That's a good idea!" Louise chimed in agreement.

But Sarah didn't think so.

"We only have enough for us," she said sadly. It was their last day of camping, so it was the last of the breakfast food.

"That's why we're going to share," said her dad. "That way, we can all have some. It's better than us having a lot and them having nothing."

Sarah hung her head. She didn't say anything else, because everyone else had already decided. She knew that Mom would have a talk with her if she had kept trying to say no.

Everyone then proceeded to help dad with the breakfast, except for Sarah. She sat by the fire and watched while her family happily worked. After a little while, she heard new voices. It was the family from the other campsite. They looked very nice, and their little girl was about her age. Still, she just couldn't be excited about giving up her favorite breakfast to strangers. Sarah didn't say hello, but instead went inside the tent.

Her mom walked up to the tent after a few minutes. "Sarah, don't you want some breakfast? It's ready. You should come meet our new friends."

Sarah came out of the tent. She wanted to make sure she had enough food. She stayed away from the new family as she picked out her breakfast. Her mom had told her to only take a little bit of food, but Sarah didn't listen. She got two big pancakes, two pieces of bacon, and a big cup of hot chocolate. Then, she took her plate and sat by the fire.

"Hi," a voice said, shyly.

Sarah looked over and saw the little girl standing there with a plate. She only had half of a pancake and a single piece of bacon. Her cup only had water in it.

"Can I sit next to you?" the girl asked.

Sarah nodded and moved over. The girl sat down next to her.

"I'm Lara," she said with a small smile. She turned to her plate and took a big bite of blueberry pancake. Even though she just had a little, she looked so excited.

"I'm Sarah," Sarah said. Suddenly, she didn't feel very hungry, and the smell of hot chocolate didn't seem as good as usual.

"I was really sad when Dad told me we wouldn't have breakfast today, but I'm so excited now! Your family is really nice."

Sarah felt really bad. When she looked around, everyone had less food than her, but they looked a lot happier than she felt. Maybe she should try to share too.

Sarah held out her hot chocolate toward Lara. "Do you want this hot chocolate? I think I took the rest of it."

Lara grinned. "Really? Are you sure?"

Her excitement made Sarah smile. "Yeah. Here." She handed it over and Lara began drinking noisily. Sarah laughed. "You can have a piece of bacon and a pancake too. I took too much."

"It's your food," Lara said. "I think you can have however much you want!"

"But I want to share," said Sarah, feeling much better already. She put a pancake on Lara's plate and gave her a piece of bacon too.

And even though Sarah didn't have as much food as she normally did, she made a new friend, and everyone said afterwards, including Sarah, that it was the best camping breakfast they had ever had.

Moral of the Story

Sarah didn't want to share her food with other people. She thought that it was her food, so she should be able to eat it and do what she wanted with it. But when she saw how disappointed Lara was, she decided to share. Sometimes, it's hard to share and be generous with what's yours. But when you share with people who have less than you have, not only will it make you happy, but it also makes the other person happy too. Who knows? Like, Sarah, you may just make a new friend too!

10: The Masterpiece

It was a hot day to have P.E. class outside, but Kiana didn't mind. She liked having a big field of grass to play on. Today, her class was playing soccer. Kiana was on a team with a lot of her friends, and they were winning!

"Wow!" Kiana exclaimed to her friend Anna who had just scored a goal. "You are so good at this!"

"Thank you!" Anna replied. "The next time we get the ball, I'll pass it to you, okay?"

"Okay!"

Kiana waited for her team to get the ball. Finally, Anna got it, and she kicked it to Kiana. Kiana saw the goal in front of her and kicked the ball really hard.

But she missed.

Kiana watched the ball hit the edge of the goal and bounce away. She hung her head and tried not to cry.

"It's okay!" said Anna. "Everyone misses sometimes. You'll get it next time."

Kiana tried to smile. She didn't believe that what Anna said was true. The thing was, Anna made the soccer team this year, and Kiana didn't. Kiana didn't even like soccer very much, but she wanted to be on the team so she could be with her friends. She liked drawing better than sports, which was why she was in the art club.

Even after Kiana missed the goal, her team still won. Her three friends on the soccer team, Anna, Jane, and Mackenzie, made almost all of the goals. Kiana felt like she didn't get to do anything.

When she went home after school that day, Kiana decided that she wanted to draw. She liked to draw when she felt sad. Most of the time, when she drew a happy picture, she felt better when it was done.

Dad knocked on her door and looked into the room. "What are you up to in here?" he asked.

"Just drawing," Kiana replied. She showed him her picture of a train going down the track on a sunny day.

"Wow! That's amazing!" He grinned. "You are so talented, Kiana."

Kiana smiled. Dad always said that. But today, she wanted to be good at soccer rather than good at art.

"Dad?" she asked. "Why am I not good at soccer when all of my friends are?"

Her dad sat down next to her. He had a handful of grapes and Kiana stole one with a giggle. Dad smiled.

"Why do you think you're not good at soccer?"

"I didn't make the team. And today, when we were playing in P.E., everyone was so much better than me. I missed a goal."

"I'm sorry, Kiana." Her dad hugged her and looked into her eyes. "I know it can hurt when it feels like you can't do something as well as someone else. But what about this?" He held up her drawing. "Can your friends do this?"

Kiana thought about it. "I don't think so."

Her dad gave the picture back to her. "I think you should take this picture to school tomorrow and show it to your friends. See what they think about it."

Kiana didn't know how that would make her feel better about soccer, but she listened to her dad anyway. The next day at school, she showed her friends the train drawing.

"This is so good!" Mackenzie said, holding it up. She stared at the drawing with big eyes.

"I can't draw like that," Jane said.

"You're really good at art," Anna said. "No wonder you're in Art Club."

"I bet it's way better than getting stinky in the hot sun all afternoon at soccer practice," Jane said, laughing.

"Well, sometimes Mrs. Moore loses her glasses. We have to spend most of Art Club finding them!" Kiana giggled.

This made all her friends laugh. Kiana thought that maybe it didn't really matter whether she was on the soccer team with her friends or not. She and her friends still had fun together. She liked the way that they could play soccer so well, and they liked the way she could draw so well.

Kiana went home happy that day. As soon as she got in the car, her dad asked her, "So, what did your friends think of your drawing?"

"They loved it!" Kiana said.

"I knew they would. Even if you're not a soccer player, Kiana, you're a true artist. Look at how your art makes people happy!"

Kiana looked at her picture again. She smiled. Dad was right.

Moral of the Story

Kiana wished she could play soccer like her friends did. But when she showed off her picture, she realized that her friends liked her unique talent. Do you know that everyone has different talents? Some people might be better at sports, some people might be better at art, and some people might be better at other things too! Love your own talent and use it to bring happiness to the people around you.

11: Trouble at the Treehouse

Tabitha was very good at making friends. She liked to talk to anyone and everyone! That was why she knew her cousins so well, even though she only saw them once a year. The only cousin she didn't really know was Ashley. Ashley was the same age as Tabitha, but she was very shy. Every time Tabitha tried to talk to her, she didn't say anything back.

So Tabitha played with her other cousins when they came to her house every year. This year, they were playing in the treehouse in the backyard. Tabitha and her cousins Will, James, and Alexandra, climbed up and down a rope that was tied to the inside of the treehouse. They picked oranges from the tree and made a pile of them inside.

Instead of playing with everyone, Ashley just watched them from the side. Tabitha brought her an orange and Ashley smiled.

"Do you want to go in the treehouse with us?" Tabitha asked.

Ashley shook her head.

"It's safe up there."

Ashley just shook her head again and began peeling her orange.

Tabitha decided that she just didn't want to play. She went back to the rest of her cousins and started up a game. They put together an obstacle course in the backyard. At the end, they had to climb up into the treehouse. Tabitha had so much fun that she forgot about Ashley watching them.

"Come play with us, Ashley!" Will said.

Ashley shook her head.

"I already asked her," Tabitha said. "She doesn't want to play."

"Why not?" Alexandra asked.

Ashley didn't answer. She just shrugged.

"You should play with us!" said James, walking over to Ashley. He took her hand and started to pull her out of her seat. "You have to go up into the treehouse."

Tabitha didn't like the way that James was pulling Ashley. "Stop it, James," she said. "It's okay if Ashley doesn't want to play."

"No it's not," Will said. "She never wants to play anything. She will like the treehouse when she gets up there."

Alexandra nodded. Tabitha looked at Ashley. Her eyes were big and she just looked scared.

"Stop!" Tabitha said. But now, all three of her cousins were pushing Ashley to the treehouse. "I'm going to tell Aunt Abigail!"

Will crossed his arms. "If you tell our mom, we will never let you play with us ever again."

Tabitha didn't know what to do. She really liked playing with her cousins, but she didn't think that they should be forcing Ashley to play with them.

Tabitha turned to look at Ashley, and realized that there were tears on her face.

That did it. Tabitha turned around and ran into the house. Even though all of the adults were eating and talking, Tabitha found her Aunt Abigail quickly.

"Tabitha?" her aunt asked as Tabitha ran up to her. "What's wrong?"

"Will, James, and Alexandra are forcing Ashley to play when she doesn't want to. I tried to tell them to stop, but they won't listen to me."

Aunt Abigail frowned. "Thank you for telling me. Will you show me where they are?"

Tabitha took Aunt Abigail out to the backyard. Ashley was back in her chair and Tabitha's three cousins were playing in the treehouse again.

Tabitha knew that they were trying to make it look like they hadn't done anything wrong. "They were pulling her to the treehouse," she told Aunt Abigail.

Aunt Abigail looked at Ashley. The little girl was still crying and sucking on her thumb.

"Are you okay, Ashley?" Aunt Abigail asked.

Ashley shook her head slowly.

"What's wrong?" James asked. He climbed down from the treehouse.

Aunt Abigail looked at him. "Tabitha told me you were forcing Ashley to play with you when she didn't want to."

"No!" said Alexandra, who came right behind James. "We asked her and she said no."

"That's not what happened," Tabitha said.

Will climbed down last. He looked mad when he saw Tabitha. "We didn't do anything," he said.

Aunt Abigail turned to Ashley again. "Did they?"

Ashley looked up at Aunt Abigail. Then, she looked at Tabitha. She pulled her thumb from her mouth and said, "Tabitha is telling the truth."

Everyone was amazed. Ashley actually talked!

Aunt Abigail stared at Will, James, and Alexandra. "Is that true?"

"I'm sorry!" Alexandra said, bursting into tears.

"We just wanted Ashley to play with us," James whined.

"She never plays with us," added Will.

"It's never okay to force someone to do something that they don't want to do," Aunt Abigail said. "And it's also never okay to lie. All three of you will go inside for a time-out."

Hanging their heads, Will, James, and Alexandra walked inside. Aunt Abigail's face was a little kinder as she looked down at Tabitha.

"You did the right thing, Tabitha. Thank you for being brave enough to come and get me."

Tabitha smiled. She walked over to Ashley. "Now that they are gone, do you want to play with me?"

Ashley's tears went away. She grinned and nodded.

And so Tabitha and Ashley drew with chalk on the sidewalk. After a little while, Will, James, and Alexandra came outside and said they were sorry to Ashley.

Ashley smiled at them. "It's okay," she said. "I forgive you."

Will, James, and Alexandra looked a lot happier after that. They took some chalk and added to Tabitha and Ashley's drawings. Tabitha watched them just in case, but they were kind to Ashley for the rest of the day.

From then on, Tabitha never saw her cousins be mean to Ashley again when they came to visit each year.

Moral of the Story

Tabitha knew that something was wrong when her cousins started forcing Ashley to play with them. She knew that if she told an adult, her cousins might not be friends with her anymore. But, because she knew it was the right thing to do, she told an adult anyway. You can be brave just like Tabitha! If you see something that doesn't look right, you have the power to tell somebody and keep bad things from happening.

Conclusion

Even though we've come to the end of the book, know that growing as a person does not stop here.

Just like the characters in each of the stories, know that growing and learning is a continuous and ongoing process!

As long as we have the strength to admit our mistakes, the courage to try again, and the boldness to take a chance, anything is possible.

We hope that you've been inspired by these beautiful stories. Hopefully, they've made a difference in the way you view things and people around you too.

Regardless of whatever comes your way, just remember:

You are unique and you can achieve anything!

Free Bonus (reminder)

Don't forget to grab the first two eBooks of our flagship Inspired Inner Genius series for free!

Simply visit: https://go.inspiredinnergenius.com/ebook or scan the QR code below to grab two inspirational biography books for your little one(s). You'll love them!